Metaphor

Art and Nature of Language and Thought

Emilio Rivano Fischer

authorHOUSE®

AuthorHouse™
1663 Liberty Drive
Bloomington, IN 47403
www.authorhouse.com
Phone: 1-800-839-8640

First published by AuthorHouse 3/18/2011

ISBN: 978-1-4567-3635-4 (e)
ISBN: 978-1-4567-3138-0 (sc)

Library of Congress Control Number: 2011901347

Printed in the United States of America

Table of Contents

Preface vii

I   Traits and Definition 1

II   Pairings..7

III Infinite Expression and the Mental 15

IV Metaphorical Symphonies 25

V   Origins and Meanings 37

VI Duality and Beyond....................................49

VII Knowledge...59

Preface

Metaphor permeates expert as well as everyday language and thought. While there is a considerable body of specialized articles and academic books on the subject, the topic matters to all branches of knowledge and to every sphere of human understanding and expression. It is important to present it plainly and free from heavy philosophical, cognitive, and linguistic theorizing. That is the main purpose of this text, which furthers on a previous book of mine, *Seven Lessons on Metaphor* (2002).

The guiding lines of the treatment of metaphor found in this book come mainly from the ideas of Mark Johnson, George Lakoff, Mark Turner, and others working in similar veins. I will mention here three of their books on the subject: Lakoff and Johnson's *Metaphors We Live By* (1980), Johnson's *Death is the Mother of Beauty: Mind, Metaphor, Criticism* (1987), and Lakoff and Turner's *More than Cool Reason*

(1989), all from The University of Chicago Press. The present text, however, differs from these books in many ways: in its primary audience and form of presentation, its scope of work and purpose, some specific ideas, and the general evaluations reached on the different topics. It also differs in the assessments made on the quality of its concepts and on the status of the knowledge acquired.

Starting with Aristotle, many other authors, writing from different perspectives, may be acknowledged on a topic as classic as this. Here, I will only mention two enduring sources: Kenneth Burke, who has given us deep and creative thoughts on the subject throughout his production, and my father, Juan Rivano, from whom I learned my first lessons on metaphor.

I

Traits and Definition

1. *What is a metaphor?*

Better than attempting a definition of the term or a description of the thing up front is to show some metaphors and then talk about what they might be. Here are a handful of them:

a. Someone says to his or her beloved: "You are the light of my life", "You are a treasure", "You are the sugar in my coffee", "You and I will sail together through life".

b. Someone says, angrily, to another: "Do you have half a brain?"

c. An old sage says in a movie: "Life has run out like a river and now I meet the Great Ocean".

We read in the newspaper: "Politics is like a game: some win, some lose".

d. We read in a book: "Atoms are really gravitational fields, like planetary systems, only of the smallest proportion known". We hear in a talk: "The mind is a computer of incredible complexity and capacity".

2. The above are metaphorical expressions. Can we now tell what a metaphor is? Could we point to it, if we saw a new one?

But these expressions are fairly normal. What is it that we are supposed to have noticed here?

Notice:

a. In the expression "you are the light of my life" the speaker is not really talking about light.

b. In the expression "you are a treasure" the speaker is not talking to a treasure, nor is he talking about a treasure.

c. In the expression "you are the sugar in my coffee" the speaker does not mean that the beloved is sugar and dissolves, therefore, in water, and can be ingested.

d. In the expression "we will sail together through life" the speaker is not saying that "life" is the name of an ocean, and that the couple will sail that ocean.

e. In the expression "Do you have half a brain?" the speaker does not imply that the person in question might only have one half of his brain inside his head.

f. In the expression "life has run like a river and now I meet the Great Ocean", the character does not say that life is a liquid that has run down from the mountains, and that he will now flow into an ocean.

g. In the expression "politics is like a game: some win, some lose" the journalist does not mean that you need a board and dice and special instructions to play the game "politics", or that you need racquets of a certain kind to do it.

h. In the expression "atoms are really gravitational

fields, like planetary systems, only of the smallest proportion known" the writer does not mean to say that in the atoms there are planets where life could be found.

i. In the expression "the mind is a computer of incredible complexity and capacity" the speaker is not saying that if we open someone's head, we will find in there a computer.

3. Notice:

a. We understand metaphors. The expressions in section 1 make perfect sense to us and sound as normal as any other normal expression. These expressions pass unnoticed.

b. We agree on the negatives given in section 2, as to what these expressions *do not* mean.

c. What these expressions do not mean is something that they nonetheless say. We know, however, that they mean something else.

4. Maybe we could answer the question of what a metaphor is if we could find some trait or traits that all metaphorical expressions have in common.

What, if anything, do the expressions in section 1 have in common, so as to deserve having a common name? What justifies calling them metaphors?

One thing we noticed was that these expressions have in them words that say things, but, really, the expressions mean something else. Could this be the trait we were looking for? In that case, we would have reached a first definition:

A metaphor is an expression that says one thing, but means something else.

We found a common trait, and we placed it in the definition.

But, are we satisfied with the method used to acquire the definition? And are we satisfied with this definition? The definition gives us a common function presumably performed by these expressions. How well does it settle the matter? Does it give us knowledge of what we wanted to know?

This procedure to reach a definition amounts to finding a common trait and stating it as the defining characteristic of metaphor. True, that's it. Questions like: "Is this how we get a definition of things?",

"What did we find, anyway?", "What kind of trait did we find?", "What does "say one thing and mean something else" mean?", "Is it really a common trait all metaphors share?", those are questions our procedure is not addressing. They are important questions, but will be addressed more profitably once we have advanced a few more miles into this new territory of metaphor.

5. So far, we have seen examples of things that the term metaphor names. These are kinds of expressions. They seemed normal, so we wanted to know what it was that made them metaphorical. A trait found is that these expressions say one thing, but mean something else. The trait is produced automatically when we speak, and passes unnoticed in everyday communication. The use of metaphor is spontaneous: We create and understand metaphorical expressions without having to reflect on them, just like any other regular form of speech.

A first definition was reached, but, we wondered, are we any wiser now about what a metaphor is? The definition stated a common trait, but the meaning and the nature of the trait remain mysterious.

II

Pairings

1. Someone says: "You are such a cold person!" We understand the expression to mean that the person is being accused of something bad; maybe, of not showing his or her emotions as normal people would; maybe, of being too calculating when it comes to human relations, or not reacting compassionately, or not getting involved in issues of common good or ideals; or maybe the person is being accused of being mean to others. All these meaning nuances and many more are possible implications of or interpretations for this expression. They share something in common, besides being something bad and unwanted, namely, they all refer to feelings: The expression accuses someone of not having the proper feelings, maybe even of having bad, undesirable, reproachable ones.

We know, without even thinking about it, that the expression does not mean that the person is being described as having low body temperature. So what happened here? How come we understand that the word "cold" does not refer to temperature in this expression, but to feeling?

What *happened* was a metaphor: the understanding of one realm of reality, in this case FEELING, in terms of another realm of reality, in this case TEMPERATURE.

We can call these combinations "pairings". Thus, we can say that in a metaphor a certain pairing takes place between two realms of reality. For example, we can speak of the FEELING-TEMPERATURE pairing in the expression above, or, simply, the FEELING AS TEMPERATURE metaphor.

Just like with definitions, when writing down a pairing, the target or main realm goes first, in this case FEELING. This is the realm that's being shaped or defined in terms of another realm, in this case, TEMPERATURE, which is the shaping or defining realm. We may write the names of realms in capital letters, so as to highlight them, and make clear that they belong to a special vocabulary about metaphors.

2. Thus, the question "what is the metaphor in the expression x" can now be rephrased as "what realms are being paired in the expression x?"

For example:

a. What is the metaphor in the expression "a healthy society"? Well, we have the realm SOCIETY and the realm HEALTH. So, we can answer that the expression works with the SOCIETY-HEALTH metaphor. The knowledge realm of HEALTH is shaping the realm of SOCIETY. Among other options, we might choose to call this the SOCIETY AS HEALTH, SOCIETY AS ORGANISM, SOCIETY AS PERSON, or SOCIETY AS PATIENT metaphor.

b. What is the metaphor in the expression "in the middle of life"? We have the realm of LIFE and the realm of TRAJECTORIES (traveled distances, with initial, middle and end points; PATHS, for the same). So we can answer that in this expression the LIFE-TRAJECTORY metaphor is at work. LIFE is being shaped in terms of TRAJECTORY. We might choose to call this the LIFE AS TRAJECTORY, LIFE AS ROUTE, LIFE AS PASSAGE, or LIFE AS JOURNEY metaphor, among other potentially suitable names.

3. What metaphors are involved in each of the following expressions? That is, what realms are being paired in them?

    a. "I can't think anymore. My mind is empty!"
    b. "May you have a long and fruitful life"
    c. "You are the sunshine of my life"
    d. "Jessica devours books"
    e. "We humans feed on knowledge"
    f. "What you say is very obscure!"
    g. "I see what you mean!"
    h. "She is a close friend"
    i. "He's got a loose screw"
    j. "Summer is coming!"
    k. "Einstein is the father of modern physics"
    l. "You are wasting my time!"
    m. "That was a heavy thought!"

Rendering the right kind of answer to the above

might not be easy at first. Maybe the realms involved don't come to mind. As with everything else, with practice, the discovery of metaphors in expressions, paragraphs, speeches, and other texts, will become increasingly easier.

3.1. Here are some first answers to the above:

The first expression pairs MIND with CONTAINER WITH OBJECTS (like a box with things inside). The mind is phrased and understood as a container of ideas, thoughts, images and whatever else we may think we have "in the head". These are the objects inside the container.

The second pairs LIFETIME with LENGTH and also LIFE with FRUIT TREE.

Expression (c) above pairs, perhaps, HAPPINESS and SUNLIGHT. But a number of other interpretations are possible. For sunshine is vital to plants, and thus, the expression could be pairing VITAL AFFECTIVE NEED (TO HUMANS) with SUN LIGHT NEED TO PLANTS.

Expression (d) pairs READING with EATING, and, perhaps, LEARNING with EATING.

(e) pairs KNOWLEDGE with FOOD, and, thus LEARNING with EATING.

(f) pairs SPEECH CLARITY with DEGREE OF LIGHT, and, thus, UNDERSTANDING with SEEING.

(g) pairs UNDERSTANDING with SEEING.

(h) pairs QUALITY OF PERSONAL RELATION (FRIENDSHIP) with DEGREE OF PROXIMITY.

(i) pairs MIND SANITY with MACHINE ASSEMBLY.

(j) pairs TIME PASSAGE with MOVEMENT TOWARD (AND AWAY FROM) POINT IN SPACE.

(k) pairs THEORY FOUNDER with FAMILY BUILDER.

(l) pairs TIME with RESOURCE.

Finally, expression (m) pairs THOUGHTS with WEIGHTS, and, thus, THINKING with CARRYING (OR SUPPORTING) WEIGHTS.

3.2. We notice that the pairings are delivered on a level of generality above that of the expression. That is, the expressions are more specific than the metaphors that they convey.

For instance, expression (k) mentions "Einstein" and "physics", but the pairing or metaphor given for expression (k) mentions THEORY BUILDER. Theories can be of any science or field of knowledge, not only of physics, and anyone can be the builder of a theory, not only Einstein. Thus, Darwin can be said to be "the progenitor of modern biology". This expression belongs to the same metaphor as the expression "Einstein is the father of modern physics", namely, the THEORY BUILDER AS FAMILY BUILDER metaphor.

Expression (m) mentions "heavy", but the pairing mentions WEIGHTS. Weights can be of any sort, not only heavy. They can be light, very light, very heavy, unnoticeable, diminishing, appalling, manageable, uncomfortable, and so on.

Expression (j) mentions "summer", but the metaphor given mentions TIME.

The pairing or metaphor is saying something more

general than the expression. The pairing implies that the expression is only one particular instance of it, among other such instances.

Thus, for instance, the SOCIETY-HEALTH pairing not only accounts for the expression "a healthy society", but also for expressions like "a sick society", "a society in need of care", "a deteriorating society", "a society growing strong", "a society in shock", "social surgery", "a society that can't breathe", "a compulsive society", "a dying society", among infinite other expressions produced in the same SOCIETY-HEALTH frame. Thus, we understand effortlessly when someone says that "knowledge and education are essential vitamins for a society". The SOCIETY-HEALTH pairing is behind that automatic understanding.

III
Infinite Expression
and
the Mental

1. Someone says: "I cannot find my way out of this problem!"

We know problems are not mazes. We know problems are not places. Problems have no doors, paths, entrances, exits, or barriers that stop you from moving forward.

Yet, somehow, we can say things like the following:

"This problem is the worst maze I've ever been in!"

"The Theory of Relativity is a jungle"

"Let's enter this problem by its main access, and

walk the path to its solution by taking each step at a time"

"Our problem is thorny. If we encounter obstacles in our path, we'll deal with them as new places that have to be entered, passed through, and exited successfully, one by one; and only after we exit each of these in our way can we return to the main road that will lead us to the final exit and to the solution of the central problem."

We said we knew that problems were not mazes or places of any other sort. Yet, we used mainly place related words in the expressions above, and they all make sense.

You can surely think of other expression in this PROBLEM-PLACE pairing. There is actually no limit to this possibility. For PLACE is a concept where infinite expression is possible, and so is then the PROBLEM AS PLACE metaphor.

2. So now we see that a metaphor is really something much bigger than an expression. A metaphor is not an expression, but something that contains, produces and explains expressions. For all the expressions above belong to one and the same metaphor. They are included in the metaphor. They are all products of the same pairing.

In this PROBLEM AS PLACE metaphor, then, countless metaphorical expressions are produced.

3. The following is an exercise designed to make you create your own expressions within a metaphor, and thus make you aware of the structure of metaphor in your own language:

In section 3.1. of Chapter II a few pairings were proposed to account for different expressions. For instance, the MIND AS CONTAINER WITH OBJECTS metaphor or pairing accounted for the expression "my mind is empty", and the LIFE TIME AS LENGTH metaphor accounted for the expression "long life".

Find in your own language three or four additional expressions for each of the pairings given in that section. That is, think out or imagine expressions that you think also are metaphorical expressions of the pairing.

4. Metaphors, then, are not the expressions, but, rather, something "behind" the expressions, something that produces them, accounts for them, and makes them understandable. The PROBLEM AS PLACE metaphor, for example, is behind the expression "you got yourself into this mess. Now you have to think of a way to get out of it". It makes us understand it, if we happen to hear it. It's what allows us to produce it, should we happen to say it.

But things are not totally clear yet. For example, you said "let's call this pairing the PROBLEM-PLACE metaphor. Do you mean we can call it different names? How do we know when we called it the right name, then?

You also said that "metaphors are behind the expressions", that they "produce the expressions", "account for the expressions", and "make them understandable". What does all this mean? How does all this happen?

The first two questions can be answered in a relatively satisfactory way, the other ones, less so. The first two have to do mainly with wording, the others, with facts.

5. The first question is: Can one and the same metaphor have different names? The answer is: Yes. For example, the PROBLEM AS PLACE metaphor could have been called the PROBLEM AS AREA metaphor.

Both PLACE and AREA are terms that refer in a similarly general way to any space with borders and other properties. Both terms can be used to refer to the kind of knowledge that we have of different kinds of places, which is what matters in this metaphor.

Other, more specific names are also possible, names that highlight different aspects of the general pairing. We call it PROBLEM AS PLACE, because PLACE is a general term that covers most options of the general concept or knowledge behind the pairing. For PLACE covers any sort of place (rooms, caves, mountains, acres, forests, buildings, houses, etc.). But the metaphor could have been called the PROBLEM AS MAZE metaphor, or the PROBLEM AS ENCLOSURE metaphor, or the PROBLEM AS TERRITORY metaphor, or maybe the PROBLEM AS JAIL metaphor. It all depends on what kind of place is being used in the expression to talk about problems, and whether we want to pay attention to this more specific knowledge realm.

The choice of a name for the metaphor will depend on the expression or text that one is trying to analyze or produce and the purpose of the analysis or product. The name, in any case, is not important in itself.

What matters is to realize the general metaphorical idea behind the expression or text under scrutiny or under design. The name of the metaphor points to the general and complex transference of knowledge involved in the metaphor, from the shaping to the shaped realm.

And we can see better now why it is a good idea to write the names of the two realms of a metaphor in capital letters: the names are not really meant as normal words, but as the proper name of the combination of two knowledge complexes. The two realms written together in the pairing are the name of the metaphor as a whole.

Well, if that was the easy answer, maybe we don't want to hear the tough one!

You are right. We better leave the other questions for later on. The above tried to answer the question of how to name a metaphor; what criteria or principles to follow; how to know when the right name has been given to a metaphor; why is the name written all in capital letters; what is the nature of this name. Answers to these questions can be worked out in different ways, and many more and deeper comments are possible, and some will surface as we move forward, but the main points surrounding the issue of the name of a metaphor have been stated.

6. The other questions, the tough ones, went over to the topic of what it meant to say that a metaphor stands "behind" the expressions: Where is it then? How do metaphors operate or function so as to "make expressions possible"? In what sense do they "account for the expressions" and "make them understandable"?

We should leave these questions for later sections. But we may say up front that we know nothing about what metaphors correspond to on a neurological level, if anything. That would require us to know a lot more about the brain than we actually do. And even if we did know more about how neurons behaved when metaphors are at work, we would still need to figure out a theory that made those new facts become part of an explanation of all that we do know about metaphors in human languages. (Not unlikely, the expression "when metaphors are at work" is assuming too much, for it implies that the brain operates one way when producing or understanding metaphors, and differently when producing non-metaphorical expressions.)

What we know about metaphors we have observed and inferred from linguistic evidence. That is the kind of object that interests the study of metaphor. The neurological statements about brain states when metaphor is being processed will, when and if accessible, matter to the discussion of certain causal constructs, but they will not matter to metaphor as a whole.

So far, what we have, given the facts, is a relatively coherent first description of the mechanism involved in metaphor. The description is compatible with the facts and tells the following story around them:

Metaphor is a mental process in which one realm of knowledge is used for the understanding of another realm of knowledge. This process leaves clear evidence of its existence in the expressions of a language. Thus, for example, the knowledge we humans have around the realm of HEALTH is used for understanding (and shaping in words) the realm of SOCIETY. We see this in expressions like "a healthy state", "this economy is the kind of medicine the country needs", "this society is sick", "we have to recover from the social moral disease that affects our land", "we have the muscle to lead the way", among infinite other expressions within the basic HEALTH-SOCIETY pairing. The HEALTH-SOCIETY pairing is the mechanism that produces those expressions and makes them understandable.

IV

Metaphorical Symphonies

1. Metaphor is all over. There is no special place to look for a metaphor. They are everywhere: in our everyday conversations with friends, at home, at work, in books, magazines and newspapers, on TV, in the movies, in public speeches. Moreover, they are not isolated events, but occur simultaneously and in rich, spontaneous, and unpredictable variety. Our common speech is full of natural metaphorical symphonies.

Let's look at the following example. It is an article about teenage love and some of its effects, particularly from psychological, sociological and educational perspectives. We will, however, not "read" the article as such, but only study metaphorical aspects of its language in this, its first paragraph:

> *When they fell in love, she was barely into her teens, and he wasn't much older. Some saw a star-crossed couple who found understanding, joy and maturity in each other's arms. Others saw impulsive kids whose reckless passion cut them off from family, friends and more appropriate interests, provoked mood swings, delinquent behavior and experimentation with drugs, and ended in tragedy. (The_New York Times, Tuesday, November 13, 2001: D6; By Winfred Gallagher "Young Love: The Good, the Bad and the Educational".)*

2. Note: "they fell in love".

This expression talks of love as some place you fall into. Thus, we have a LOVE AS END POINT OF FALL metaphor here. Now, a first reading for the term "fall" is something unexpected, an accident. The result of this accident, further on, is generally something bad: an injury of some sort. Of course, you may fall on cotton, but, generally speaking, it is better not to fall, than to fall. There is also a sense of the inevitable: once falling, there is not much you can do about it. Love, then, in as much as it is thought through the lenses of this metaphor, and only through them, (a strategy, that would have left us without mammoth, and perpetually running from saber tooth), would be conceived as an accidental, inescapable, dangerous, and maybe harmful event. Thus, metaphors like the following also come to mind: LOVE AS ACCIDENT, LOVE AS DISEASE, and LOVE AS TRAP.

The expression "to fall in love", it must be pointed out, is a rather isolated member in both the LOVE AS END POINT OF FALL metaphor (or, LOVE AS TRAP metaphor) and the LOVE AS ACCIDENT metaphor. For other expressions which would be thought to run naturally out of these pairings, such as "I climb on the roots to get out of this love", "high-mountain skills is all I used to get out of that love", "he fell in love, but bounced right back", "he had a special tool that took him out of the love-trap", sound quite strange. And the same seems true of expressions like "the love ambulance came to that accident", "that guy is in love, so bring some first aid here", and "I recovered from that love with these new anti-love pills", and so on.

Thus, the negative undertones suggested by metaphors such as LOVE AS END POINT OF FALL, and LOVE AS ACCIDENT, which underlie the expression "to fall in love", are rather marginal, all in all.

3. Note: "…she was barely into her teens".

Here, we have the ages as places that we go into. The TIME AS PLACE metaphor is responsible for our talking of time from such a wide variety of perspectives that it should better be called a macro-metaphor. The still more general TIME AS SPACE metaphor allows us to divide time, measure time, pass through time, be in time, be at the same time, and infinite other specific operations we unconsciously carry out as normal ways of organizing ourselves and the world in the dimension of time.

4. Note: "Some saw a star-crossed couple who found understanding, joy and maturity in each other's arms".

Of course, "saw" here means "conceived", "understood".

The expression "a star-crossed couple", a version of the

idiom "star-crossed lovers", means lovers doomed by the stars to fail. Shakespeare coined it for the ill-fated Romeo and Juliet.

Furthermore, the sentence contains a specification of some objects found by the couple: They "found understanding, joy and maturity in each other's arms". They found very valuable things. Thus, there has been a search, a journey, and the travelers have been lucky in that respect, but unlucky in the heavenly design of their joined destiny.

Some metaphors involved in this:

UNDERSTANDING AS SEEING
(LOVE) DESTINY AS HEAVENLY DESIGN
LOVE AS OBJECT
LOVE AS RESOURCE
LOVE AS SEARCH FOR VALUABLE OBJECTS
LOVE AS JOURNEY

5. Note: "Others saw impulsive kids whose reckless passion cut them off from family, friends and more appropriate interests, provoked mood swings, delinquent behavior and experimentation with drugs and ended in tragedy."

In "impulsive kids" the term "kid" is literally and metaphorically a diminishing figure. An adolescent is not a kid; and this, in several respects that make them more independent and powerful than kids: they run faster, they hit harder, they know more, they are stronger and taller, they can articulate their own will and ideas in language, etc. The adult-kid relation is conceived of as care-taking. Now, if these kids are "impulsive", it means that they cannot control their will, and, since they are not really kids, this is dangerous.

"…whose reckless passion cut them off from family, friends and more appropriate interests": The enemies (or evil doers) are some uncaring, inconsiderate passions, who perform by "cutting off" a few valuable and vital ties, thus leaving the kids without them, and the ties without the kids. These passions also perform by causing "…mood swings, delinquent behavior and experimentation with drugs".

Some metaphors of this include:

PASSIONS AS WRONGDOER
PASSIONS AS WOODCUTTER
RELATIONSHIPS AS BRANCHES

RELATIONSHIPS AS TIES
PERSONAL INTERESTS AS TIES
DISRUPTION IN RELATION AS CUTTING
OFF BRANCH
PASSION AS MISCHIEVOUS INCONSIDER-
ATE AGENT
PASSION AS CAUSE OF BAD STATES AND
DANGEROUS BEHAVIOR

6. Note: "…and ended in tragedy."

Not that *the passions* ended in tragedy, as the gram-mar of the text implies, but *the kids*, of course. Now, to come to an end is to be no longer in the path. There is here, more explicitly than in the previous view of the couple, a journey metaphor – of life, relationship, and love.

This tragic end in this negative journey contrasts with the finding of maturity in the first, positive jour-ney – maturity being also a kind of end, but an end of proper completion, the good, beneficial result of growing and nourishment.

7. Notice that we are presented with two opinions in this paragraph: one sympathetic to the couple, the other opposed to it. Both of these opinions are phrased in metaphorical language. Both agree in the fatal end of the couple, but disagree in the total evaluation of what happened and on who is to be blamed for it. The first works around images of bad heavenly design for our destinies, finding valuable objects and resources in joined journeys, and growing to beneficial completion. The other works with images of evil agents, the passions, that cut off vital branches from us, or even chop up pieces of our own bodies, move our moods, and cause evil and self destructive behavior; and the image of a tragic end of a journey.

Thus, the rhetorical dimension of making an audience identify itself with something, or making it reject something, finds a powerful resource in metaphorical language.

8. *You said in the beginning of this chapter that "We will...not "read" the article as such, but only study aspects of its language, the metaphorical aspects". Yet, it looks as if this study of the metaphorical aspects of a text is a reading. So, is this "study of the metaphorical aspects of language" a way to read a text of any kind?*

It is. In fact, it is a very effective tool when reading a text, any text: It helps us understand the text and its foundation, its assumptions, its main guiding images, and, in so doing, it opens the text to both aesthetic and critical evaluation: The imagery used is disclosed; its degree of correspondence with what we know of what is portrayed is exposed to our awareness; the inspecting, neutral eye is awakened; the general purposes of the text, whether unconscious or not, implicit or explicit, may appear more clearly as the basic images are revealed; the argumentative quality of the composition is open for a review of its terminology, its presuppositions, and its soundness.

The points the text assumes as established, unquestioned truths, as well as those it wants to establish, become concrete, visible. The linguistic strategies used to convince, to gain support, to impose a certain picture of things, to promote certain preferences and dispositions in the audience, and even produce action, those strategies are uncovered, open to inspection as the study of the metaphors of a text reveal the basic figures employed.

When I said that we would not read the article as a whole, but only study aspects of some of its metaphors, I meant that the point of the exercise was not to read the article so as to disclose its overall figurative architecture, the strategies and the points it wants to make, the number of presuppositions it contains, and the quality of its arguments, but simply to apply metaphorical analysis, so as to see it at work and start using it as a tool.

9. All sorts of texts are profitably designed or examined for their metaphorical quality, be they arguments, descriptions, scientific theories, critical essays, poems, novels, movie scripts, ads, jokes, one-liners, political speeches, or whatever, including one's own conceptions of different things.

Mctaphors are all over the place. Their functions, the jobs they do, are innumerable: They may be used for the sake of pure understanding, for the sake of flattering, for the sake of insulting, as a presupposition that functions automatically whenever we infer or reason, as a way to lead people in one direction, as a way to convince someone, as a way to rapidly figure something out, as an instrument of analysis, as a way to organize content, as a tool for designing speech, as a way to organize behavior, and so on and on. And they may be used in any combination we may think of among the above kinds of achievement. There is no limit to the list of functions and purposes in which metaphors may assist.

10. The following exercise helps you see the diversity of fields for metaphorical production and the complexity in the metaphorical structure of any text. The exercise also makes you aware of the more specific functions that metaphors may perform in language:

Find an article, a poem, a (very) short story, or any other short text (one page or so), and map out the metaphors it employs. You may organize your work and result in the manner done in this chapter, advancing expression by expression and stating a pairing, whenever there seems to be one. You may also choose to read a global metaphor in the text, and work your way down to the expressions, that is, from a global reading to the more specific images used in the text. You may also attempt a combination of the above, or any other method you may think of to present your account of the metaphors in your text.

V
Origins and Meanings

1. *But what about the word "metaphor"? It is a weird word. Where does it come from?*

"Metaphor" is Greek for "transference". The "trans" part is "meta". The "ference" part is "phor". The original Greek was *metapherein*, which better shows the link: Latin "ference" comes from Greek *pherein*.

Now, *pherein* comes from an old Indo-European root, *bher*, which means "to carry", "to bear". We can still see the same root in "bear", "born", "birth", "burden", as we can see its Latin shape in words like "refer", "confer", "defer", "differ", "infer", "suffer", "proffer", "offer", among others.

So, "metaphor" originally meant "carrying over". Aristotle was the first we know to study and define this linguistic phenomenon. We need not go into Aristotle's treatises here. But it is instructive to mention the kind of understanding he had of it. As the meaning of the word *metapherein* suggests, a metaphor was understood as a sort of carrying over of one word to the place of another word or another meaning, and, also, as a carrying of something alien by the word (the *carrier*), something that did not belong to it. Thus, for instance, the word "honey" to name "loved one" would be said to be a metaphor: the word "honey" was carried over to another place, a place different from its own and proper one, the place of "loved one", to do the job of that word, to express, carry, or bear that meaning. Aristotle was not thinking about transference of whole systems of knowledge, as we are, but only of words. One thing that would license word transference, according to Aristotle, is a common kind for the species involved. Thus, for instance, both "honey" and "loved one" are "pleasant things", and this belonging to the same kind makes the transit possible, from honey to loved one. It is fair to say that our way of understanding metaphor comes from Aristotle's first seed on the subject.

We would now rather say that the entire realm of FOOD is being paired with the realm of LOVE and also SEX, and we would view expressions like "sugar", "I'd like to eat you up", "he looks delicious", "honey", as well as "repulsive person", "he is disgusting", "bad taste", among uncountable others, as expressions within the same metaphor.

2. *I have a dictionary definition of metaphor with me. It says:*

> *Metaphor: 1. A figure of speech in which a word or phrase that ordinarily designates one thing is used to designate another, thus making an implicit comparison as in "a sea of troubles" or "all the world's a stage" (Shakespeare). (The American Heritage Dictionary of the English Language. Third Edition. 1992)*

Now that is kind of different from what we have been saying throughout these lessons, isn't it?

It is. That is a pretty standard definition of metaphor. It looks like our first definition, more or less. So, you might say that we started off from it. And you might notice Aristotle's influence. For the definition really stays at the level of words. Now, we are trying to embrace, not just single words and expressions, but whole realms of knowledge. That's more economical:

it brings more profit for less work. For, instead of going through every single metaphorical word or expression and explaining or accounting for them one by one, we jump to the general level of realms of knowledge, and account for whole lots of them in a simple and effective way. Ours is a better, more powerful tool!

The same dictionary includes a second definition of metaphor. It says:

> *2. One thing conceived as representing another; a symbol: "The high-rise garbage repository is a metaphor for both accomplishment and failure" (Richard Sever)*

Now that is really different from what we have been saying here!

Yes, it is different from what we have been saying, but not a lot different from the previous definition. It says that you can take a "thing" to symbolize something else. Like when a tall building symbolizes progress, or when a flower symbolizes love. The building, then, is said to be a metaphor for progress, and the flower, a metaphor for love. In the example of the definition, a more revealing thing was chosen, for rhetorical purposes, but the principle is the same.

And the points made before apply here too, only that, instead of words and expressions, we now have things and phenomena. For, things, taken as isolated objects, also present the shortcomings mentioned: Our account would have to go through every single thing that symbolizes something else, instead of just dealing with the whole knowledge realms involved, say, CONSTRUCTION and GROWTH.

We see also that the process whereby a thing symbolizes something else, is, many times, not a complex metaphorical operation (where two realms of knowledge pair), but a simple procedure of selecting something that is, for instance, an effect, and make it represent its cause, or make it represent the whole cause-effect process. Thus, the garbage repository is said to represent the technologically accomplished society, but is, in fact, a by-product of that society. For garbage is not really "something else", but an effect of the accomplishment and a real negative aspect of it.

3. Most people never really reflect much about the language they use at all. Now and then, the issue of the meaning of a word in a message comes up, for the message is ambiguous or obscure. Sometimes a weird pronunciation or a strange or foreign word causes communication to stop for a while. But most of the time people are totally unaware of their everyday language.

People just use language to say things without having to think about how it is that the language is constructed so as to make possible what they say. Of course, if they did stop to think about that, saber tooth would be very happy, and we would probably not be here now, talking about Aristotle and metaphor.

But *we* don't have to run from saber tooth. Not while writing or reading this, anyway. And now we know about a mechanism that is central to our common understanding of things and our way of talking. And, yet, the mechanism is mostly hidden from awareness. That's an edge. Apart from insight and pleasure, this break we took from language use will give us an advantage when using language and facing saber tooth again.

Metaphor is in the nature of language and thought.

It comes to us effortlessly. But it is also an art of language and thought. It can be detected, criticized, rejected. It can be consciously manipulated, engineered, improved.

We may tune our ear and orchestrate our tongue both to appreciate the metaphorical symphonies all around us and to better play them.

4. *We have learned a new word and its meaning. In fact, its meaning has by now been explained much longer and more precisely than that of other words, apparently at least as important, such as "friendship", "guilt", "freedom", "identity", "thought", "matter", "time", "idea", "history", "space", to name just a few. How come we don't have books and whole lessons on those words?*

Actually, we have, not about the words themselves, but about what they may stand for, their meanings. And we would find that their meanings imply many times metaphorical understandings of one kind or another. And now we have a tool that helps us identify those understandings and improve our way of talking about them.

Take "guilt". Let's say you feel guilt. You may feel, then, "as if you haven't paid a debt". There is a metaphor lurking here, pairing GUILT with DEBT. Well, say you "pay the debt" (although no real debt or payment were involved), and you "feel relieved". The feeling of guilt was a "burden". So, there is another metaphorical understanding of GUILT AS BURDEN. And this may help you understand an author or text that talks about guilt, say, from a psychological perspective, and works out the economical metaphor, and combines it with the physical weight metaphor, and draws conclusions about what guilt is, and claims to explain the mechanisms of guilt, and how to deal with it, and so on. But the text never mentions the metaphors involved, never makes explicit what the basic images are, and the fact that the basic elements were already there, in the common language, to begin with. These are just assumed. But we can now read those basic understandings. The whole text unfolds as natural ramifications of basic images. The choice of terms and their basic meanings are as clear to us as a twenty dollar bill and a pound of sugar.

Take "thought": you may "follow a thought". That means there is a metaphorical understanding that pairs THOUGHT with MOVEMENT: understanding or having a thought as moving behind someone or something through a terrain, or moving along a path. The whole activity of thinking, shaped as the activity of moving. The thought may be difficult to follow. You can find an idea in your search. You can stand on firm ground. You may have a guide that knows the terrain. You may encounter different paths as you move along. The road may split in two directions: you have a dilemma. You may have to come back to a previous point in your thinking. You may feel disoriented. You may get lost. The thought may get too deep. And so on and on.

Take "freedom". A number of basic understandings of this concept come to mind: you have metaphors that work out the escape from concealment scenery, others, the cutting off of ties, others, the exercising of control or the power of manipulation or the power of maneuvering, others exploit the images of going beyond frontiers, the trespassing of limits, the transcendence of physical boundaries, the transcendence of natural impositions (like fear, sexual impulse, hunger), others exploit the capacity to create things. Freedom is one of those concepts that interest us humans, and thus receives all sorts of attention from different metaphorical perspectives.

And in this selection of perspectives lies the rhetorical

functions of metaphor, that is, the value of metaphorical expressions as means to persuade an audience, to create opinion, to impose attitudes, to incite to action, to establish views or particular understandings of things, to activate a feeling of identity towards something, to create cohesion and acceptance in a population. For, if your interest lies in making the public accept, say, a repressive policy, when addressing freedom, you would rather work with images of control, power to manipulate, and security, than images of cutting off of ties, trespassing the limits of previous arrangements, or creating new solutions.

5. *Do all languages understand, say, "guilt" or "thought" the same way?*

That's an empirical question: we would have to find out what other languages' metaphors are. And if we did some research we would find that some metaphors are pretty widespread among the languages of the world, like TIME AS PLACE, but some aren't, like LOVE AS END POINT OF FALL. At any rate, that work is barely started. And the task is not a minor project: Throughout the societies of the world you will find metaphorical understandings of any concept that seems important to us.

Notice, to add to this density, that we don't just have one metaphor for concepts like guilt, thought, or any other abstract realm we care to think about, but scores of them.

So the question is not, really, Do all languages understand guilt and thought in the same way, but Do they understand them in the same *ways*. And *that*, they most certainly do not. Not even as English speakers can we say we all consciously understand them in the same ways. For we would manifest slightly different understandings of these abstract notions, even if we may share some common ground.

And we may deliberately choose to understand them in certain ways to the exclusion of others: Should society be a hierarchical pyramid of human roles or a collaborating human chain? Is culture nourishment or poison? Are institutions channels for individual realization or machines for individual oppression? Is work slavery or emancipation? Are people obedient and innocent sheep or wild and dangerous predators?

6. The following exercise flows naturally from this lesson: Get together with friends or anyone who knows other languages (which could be yourself), and discuss metaphors in that language or those languages. If you are lucky, these metaphors might not exist in English.

This is not an easy exercise and it should be thought of as going fishing: you might get a fish, or just have a good time trying to.

One way to go about it is to grab a bilingual dictionary and translate metaphorical expressions in English word by word to the other language, and then ask whoever knows the other language what those translations mean. You will often hit funny gibberish, meaning the metaphor might not be there like in English. If you asked a Spanish speaker how to say "that's a bright idea", you would get in response something like "es una idea brillante". And then you would be disappointed to learn that "brillante" means "bright", so that both Spanish and English (as all other European languages) make use of the UNDERSTANDING AS SEEING metaphor (and the more specific IDEA AS SOURCE OF LIGHT metaphor). So, no luck there! But if you asked how to say "he is annoying" you might get "es pesado", and you would be pleased to learn that "pesado" means "heavy", which is an unexpected concept for this meaning...

VI
Duality and Beyond

1. Let us consider one topic that relates to metaphors, present, yet not explicitly brought to our discussions in the previous Chapters. It is the topic of a general tendency that may be observed in the kind of realms involved in metaphors and the roles they play. The following list of contrasting terms captures this general tendency:

Metaphors deal with **the abstract in terms of the concrete**

("she built her own theory"; "this is a hard problem"; "a brilliant idea"; "a solid speech"; "institutional strength"; "the roads of life"; "the landmarks of history"; "a long time")

Metaphors shape **the spiritual in terms of the material**

("he showed moral resistance"; "she shows spiritual height"; "yours is a faith of steel"; "a clean spirit"; "a twisted person"; "a warm relation")

In metaphors **the mental is expressed in terms of the physical**

("you have a strong mind"; "don't hurt my feelings"; "a big intellect"; "sharp mental faculties"; "desires attract"; "a mental regression"; "an explosion of anger"; "jealousy is burning him alive")

Metaphors treat **the psychological in terms of the physiological**

("his will was dying"; "his ego is sick"; "mental health"; "mental vision"; "grasp an idea"; "swallow an idea"; "a living feeling"; "the birth of consciousness"; "a growing awareness")

The above list of antithetical or opposing terms could continue, for it contains but a few manifestations of a general dynamic feature of metaphors that unfolds in many forms, performs different functions, and serves different purposes. The above list merely names a few of those general functions, and does not go into them in more detail.

One general way to describe this feature (which accounts for the resemblance we might appreciate in the members of the list) is the following: In metaphor a relatively rich and precise realm of experience and knowledge shapes another realm, relatively less rich and less precise than the first one in experience and knowledge. These realms normally correspond to the material and the immaterial, the spiritual and the corporeal, the mental and the physical, the abstract and the concrete, the known and the mysterious, the tangible and the intangible, the natural order and the social order, and so on.

And given this short list of opposites, we may venture the suggestive following picture: In every metaphor a link is established that neutralizes the opposition at stake (the kind of oppositions in our list.)

We may also, by another image, say that in metaphor the immaterial is brought to the material, the psychological to the physiological, etc.

Thus, for instance, in the MIND AS COMPUTER

metaphor we use the realm of computers to shape the realm of mind: We know more and more precisely about computers than about the mind. After all, we make computers, but we do not make minds. Computers are material, minds are immaterial. Computers are physical, minds are mental. Thus, when viewing the mind as a computer we are guided by relatively clear landmarks in our understanding of mental phenomena. However, a mind is not a computer. But we can advance in our view of the mind if we incorporate into our efforts to understand mind the relatively precise computer notions of, for instance, "program", "information", "memory", "instruction", "process", "intelligence", "retrieval", "search", "state", "input-output", "function", "code", "machine language", "system", "algorithm", and so on.

Now, the shaping realm of the metaphor will only address certain aspects of the shaped realm, not the whole of it. And it will do so by the use of certain aspects of itself, not the whole of it. The aspects used will be those that, somehow, fit or serve or are revealing of the shaped realm. Thus, the COMPUTER realm will only address certain aspects of the realm of MIND, and it will do so by lending only some of its elements and their characteristic traits and operations.

Other traits and operations will simply be rejected as irrelevant for the realm of MIND - e.g. the fact that we use disks and CD-ROMS to store memory and programs; the fact that disks have tracks; the shape of a computer; the fact that it is plugged to a power source; the fact that we need a screen to see what we are typing and see what programs are available; the color of our PC; and so on.

2. That it should be so, that the concrete shapes the abstract, the material the immaterial, and so on, is not really surprising: we know more and know more precisely about things that are material than things that are not material; we humans can and do experience physical phenomena in a relatively similar, common way, but are on less firm ground when dealing with mental experience; we know our body and have all sorts of words for its parts and functions, but are considerably less precise about our souls, its parts and functions, so much so, that we cannot even talk about them without the help of material things and our body; we know the world of things and their properties and relations, but the world of ideas and principles, the world of psychological and spiritual states, the world of morals, all of these depend for their very formulation on the material, the physiological, the physical.

3. Other realms aligned in terms of the above are:

THE SOCIAL IS SHAPED BY THE NATURAL

THE RELIGIOUS IS SHAPED BY THE HU-MAN

THE HEAVENLY IS SHAPED BY THE EARTHLY

NEW TECHNOLOGY IS SHAPED BY OLD TECHNOLOGY

TECHNOLOGY IS SHAPED BY BODY FUNC-TION AND PART

THE MORAL DIMENSION IS SHAPED BY THE PHYSICAL

Come up with expressions in the realms of the social, the religious, the technological and the moral, and figure out the metaphors involved. You will notice the general tendency discussed in this Chapter.

4. *But wait! I think there is something mysterious here.*

*For it looks as if metaphor, or maybe our way to deal with it, is implying that there are **two** different things here, two "realms", two dimensions. And we are not alerted to see this critically and question it. I mean, what if the concrete existed, but not the abstract – that is, not as something that is not just part of the concrete. What if the material existed, but not the immaterial – that is, not as something that existed beyond the material? What if the physiological existed, but not the psychological, that is, as something different from the physiological? What if the natural existed, but not the social – as something that wasn't natural? What if metaphor is **imposing** two-sided patterns in our thinking habits?*

Those are important thoughts. Metaphor works with dualism, that is, two irreducible sides, like mind-body, spirit-matter, idea-thing, concept-experience. And metaphor works by creating bridges, pairings, between them. Metaphor makes a leap between these two irreducible sides.

Now you question whether there are two sides to these bridges. If the sides really are irreducible, what are we saying when we say that metaphor "links" them? Maybe there are bridges, but not two sides. Maybe there is the illusion of another side. We just walk from the shaping, ground level side, out to the bridge, but there is no other side. Maybe metaphor is a mental mechanism that is helpful to the point of creating certain illusions for practical purposes. Maybe deep science, real knowledge, should blow the bridge up, go beyond that mechanism that serves everyday communication and everyday knowledge, be alert against the metaphors we live by.

5. Maybe there is no soul-body or mind-brain divide. Our knowledge of the body is not only scarce, but really quite abstract when dealing with actual physiological, neurological and genetic explanations. The same goes for our knowledge of the physical or material world. What remains outside serious theorizing about reality is "mysterious", but that doesn't mean it is essentially different from other phenomena. It only means we cannot understand it.

When talking about the PROBLEM AS PLACE metaphor in expressions like "I cannot find my way out of this problem", we said we knew problems had no doors, paths, entrances, exits, or barriers that would stop us from moving forward. We said we knew a problem was not a maze or any other kind of place. Well, do we?

When we think about it, a door is not at all a square piece of wood sometimes found between rooms, but, rather, a pretty abstract notion. And it is this notion that the word "door" means, and that we *know*; not the piece of wood at all. And it is that notion that a PROBLEM actually *has*.

6. Duality is probably an inborn cognitive device. We function effortlessly in terms of quick categorizations like natural-social, body-mind, material-spiritual, physiological-mental, sensation-understanding, experience-idea, practical-theoretical, religious-worldly, concrete-abstract, and so on. This duality "gene" brings its own optics. It creates a particular perception of the world. We function perfectly well with the help of that framework. Just like we go through life well believing that the sun *rises* and *sets*, the moon is *up*, and the *line* of the horizon is *flat*. But, if we really want to know, the sun does not rise, the moon is not up, the horizon is not flat. Those are "illusions". Our first instinctive categorizations are fine to a point beyond which knowledge may start.

VII

Knowledge

1. We have now reached a position from which we can address a set of questions that have remained unanswered since Chapter I. We saw a few metaphorical expressions and asked what metaphors are. One way to address the question, we said, would be to find something in common for all those expressions. Then, I said:

> One thing we noticed was that these metaphorical expressions have in them words that say things, but, really, the expressions mean something else. Could this be the trait we were looking for? In that case, we would have reached a first definition:

A metaphor is an expression that says one thing, but means something else.

We found a common trait, and we placed it in the position of the defining sentence of the definition we were pressed to state.

Then you said:

But are we satisfied with this definition? The definition gives us a common function presumably performed by these expressions. How well does it settle the matter? Does it give us knowledge of what we wanted to know?

Then I said:

This procedure to reach a definition amounts to finding a common trait and stating it as the defining characteristic of metaphor. True. That's it. Questions like: "Is this how we get a definition of things?", "What did we find, anyway?", "What kind of trait was it that we found?", "What does "say one thing and mean something else" mean?" and "Is it really a common trait all metaphors share?", these are questions our procedure to reach a definition is not addressing.

So, let us take these questions, one by one:

Are we satisfied with this definition?

Well, we have talked about it when dealing with standard dictionary definitions of metaphor: These barely touch the surface of metaphor. They do not settle the matter, but merely start it. We ask someone who Peter is as a person, and get for reply "Peter is the boy that lives in the yellow house." Are we satisfied with this answer? We ask what a black hole is and get the answer "they are little spots in galactic space that attract and swallow everything, even light". Are we satisfied? If we want to know what black holes are, this could not be more than the beginning of our search.

Does the definition give us knowledge about metaphors?

The definition gives us a trait, and states that all metaphors share this trait, and implies that this should be enough knowledge. But it isn't. It is one piece of something, and unless you can place it in an overall scheme of things, it really doesn't give you much.

Is this how we get a definition of things?

It certainly is a very common procedure, much used in dictionaries and elsewhere for all sorts of words and notions. But we have advanced into a more comprehensive description of metaphor. Our procedure does not go after a common trait, but after the mechanism that may underlie the production and understanding of metaphorical expressions. And this mechanism should account for the fact that metaphorical expressions share certain general traits and perform certain functions.

There is a further important lesson lurking here. For, metaphors in themselves are alternative procedures to reach a definition of a notion, word or concept, a procedure different from that of finding a common trait. We saw, for instance, a number of metaphors for freedom. These are all candidates for definitions of freedom. Thus, someone may develop a definition of freedom in terms of "escape from concealment", or in terms of "the cutting off of ties", or in terms of "the exercise of control", or "the power of manipulation", or "the power of maneuvering", or "going beyond established frontiers", or "losing the sense of self", or "losing the sense of others", or "breaking old forms", or "creating new forms", and so on and on. Exploiting the resources of anyone of these basic images gives you a definition of freedom, in the sense of a relatively clear, specific and coherent determination for the notion of freedom. It also gives you an algorithm for freedom: a formula that guides you or a set of rules that tell you how to proceed.

That is a procedure for reaching definitions that is profitably followed when dealing with "those concepts that interest us humans". Combinations of basic images like the above may be attempted in more sophisticated accounts of freedom, accounts that may seek to gain wider audiences by combining many images, or may seek higher descriptive adequacy or practical efficiency by developing and refining them.

What did we find, when we found the common trait of metaphorical expressions to be that they "have in them words that say things, but, really, the expressions mean something else"?

We can say now that we found an effect of the pairing, an effect of the metaphor: The metaphorical expressions have words which are produced by and understood within a given pairing of two realms of knowledge and experience. That is their place of birth and home. So we should really rephrase this trait a little, for it is misleading to frame it as "words that say things, but mean something else." We should rather say that the words in metaphorical expressions belong to a pairing, which is a particular environment of understanding where two realms of knowledge are combined. These pairings are the mechanism that makes the words in the expressions understandable.

Is the above trait common to all metaphors?

The trait has been rephrased. We have developed considerably upon the first observations about metaphorical expressions. The first definitions and suggestions were departure points for us. We have advanced to a more insightful position, and we have reached a more complex description of the phenomenon. Things that were thought to be metaphors might not fit our description anymore. They would still be metaphors for the common language, the dictionaries and texts and other communication that might not require deeper insight. But they would not be metaphors, strictly speaking, from our framework's perspective. Thus, for instance, in an expression like "the burning flag was a metaphor for the country's state of war", we might say that there really aren't two different realms of knowledge and experience involved here. The expression is simply the manifestation of a symbol (the flag) in a state (that of burning) that is also a characteristic state of many things in a war. That is one way to use the word "metaphor", and we should have no quarrel with it. It just isn't the kind of phenomena we have accounted for.

2. Another pending issue: Back in Chapter III, a question was raised:

> *You also said that "metaphors are behind the expressions", that they "make expressions possible" that they "account for the expressions" and "make them understandable". What does all this mean? How does all this happen?*

My answer was that these were difficult questions. They ask for the explanation of it all: How does it happen? Where are the metaphors, if they are not the expressions but something "behind" expressions? How do metaphors produce understanding? What does it mean to say that one realm shapes another realm? And how was the first realm understood in the first place, anyway?

Many of these questions have no good answers. Some might never be properly answered. How is understanding possible, in the first place? That question is much too broad to be addressed seriously in one text; it might require several different theories, so far unavailable, to be properly confronted: theories of perception, of memory, of neural firings, of symbolic processing, of the language faculty, of genetics, of semantics, of logical form, of interaction patterns, to mention a few requirements; it might even be simply impossible ever to answer it. Maybe the question is not even a clear and proper question for knowledge at all, for it assumes that answers are to be provided for notions of that vague, open, ambiguous, changing, and general nature. Once studied seriously, what we call "understanding" is not one thing, but lots of things, products of mental processes that come together in innumerable combinations to produce different things and perform different functions. And all that we loosely call "understanding"; for when we use the word, in everyday language, it really isn't important to go through the mechanism responsible for the particular "understanding" at stake, but simply whether it happened or not. And, then, that's the job that word performs.

Giving an answer to what understanding is might be comparable to answering "how is anything possible?" or "what is Being?" Even if you may start off by wondering what life is, or what language is, and so on, you'll end up trying to explain smaller entities, like, how does the cell of this organ work, or what makes the sun shine weaker in the evening, or how is the vocabulary of a language acquired by the child.

We said back in Chapter III that we could tell the following story around the facts concerning metaphorical expressions:

> Metaphor is a mental process in which one realm of knowledge is used for the understanding of another realm of knowledge. This process leaves clear evidence of its existence in the expressions of a language. Thus, for example, the knowledge we humans have around the realm of HEALTH is used for understanding (and shaping in words) the realm of SOCIETY. We see this in expressions like "a healthy state", "this economy is the kind of medicine the country needs", "this society is sick", "we have to recover from that social moral disease that affects our land", "we have the muscle to

lead the way", among infinite other expressions within the basic HEALTH-SOCIETY pairing. The HEALTH-SOCIETY pairing is the mechanism that produces those expressions and makes them understandable.

That is a coherent story around the facts. It presents certain attractions: it is simple enough to understand; it is compatible with the linguistic evidence; it accounts for the metaphorical expressions by giving each its place in a given pairing; it offers unity and system in the vastly complicated dimension of the metaphorical. Each metaphorical expression is brought to this more abstract environment, the pairing, where it receives a sort of logical and genealogical place. The expression makes sense as part of a bigger whole that contains it as one of its parts, among many others; and the pairing can be said to be the origin of the metaphorical expression, for it is understood as the process that creates it.

This kind of description of metaphor and method for metaphorical analysis serves many purposes: it brings an all embracing order, a system, to the superficially chaotic diversity of metaphorical expressions; it allows one to go beyond a language, and compare different languages on these semantic dimensions; it allows you to reveal and thus examine and compare different conceptions people may have of notions and phenomena of common interest; it is a powerful tool for the analysis and design of stylistic, rhetorical, poetic, logical, and practical dimensions of all sorts of texts. The tool makes also clear that metaphors play an important role in argumentation, for they contain assumptions or premises hidden from normal inspection, which become exposed by this method. Finally, the tool may be employed skillfully to control, manipulate, and improve our use of language.

Beyond that, we encounter limits to our description. We may see that the story we have told assumes quite a few things that are not explained: What is a realm of knowledge and experience? Where does it come from? How is it formed? What is a concept? What, more precisely, is a pairing? How does a pairing create new understanding? Are pairings really pairings, that is, *two* spheres of knowledge combined? And so on. We will find that some of these questions can be partly worked out, but, for the most part, they have no clear answers, beyond the sphere of stipulation or the mention of new notions themselves in need of clarification.

3. *But, this makes me think that there are a few metaphors hidden in our account of metaphor.*

Right! First, we mentioned the metaphor in the word itself: "metaphor" means "carrying over". And this basic image guides Aristotle as well as current use to view metaphors as transference of meaning, a powerful and fruitful image.

We, ourselves, have talked of "two" and of "realms". That means we have implied countable objects. And what's a realm? Is it a place, an "environment"? We've talked in terms of "pairings"; that sounds like procreation of two to form a third. It also sounds like putting two objects together. We have talked about "images", as if mental pictures were involved in the process. We talked of the "abstract" being "shaped by" the "concrete". "Abstract" means "taken from", like a part being removed from a whole of some sort, for study or other use. "Concrete" means "grown together", "hardened". If something shapes another thing then the first is active and the second passive; the second is transformed. We also said the metaphors are "links that neutralize oppositions". Then we said that in metaphors the concrete is "brought to" the abstract, the physical to the mental, etc. This "bringing to" is an image near the original *metapherein*, "carrying over". We can go on and on with this list. Metaphor is all over our account of metaphor. And one way to evaluate the quality of the account would start by describing the main metaphors of the account itself, one by one, and then get an overall picture of their combination and what they are saying.

Any verbal communication, speech, discourse, text, treaty, description, or theory must make use of the metaphorical resources of language.

To the extent that a description of metaphor reveals real properties of things in the world (in the standard scientific senses of the words "real", "property", and "thing"), to that extent the language and images it uses and their further development, modification and specification, amount to a successful theory. That's the way our knowledge progresses. But revealing real properties and real things in the world, when dealing with the spheres of meaning, language, and thought, is a rare accomplishment.

The whole mechanism proposed as the explanation should be refined considerably, and corroborated by additional evidence, from various sides, so as to validate it as *the* human mechanism responsible for the production of metaphorical expressions. That is a very ambitious claim. So far, all we have is a coherent first story, sketching one mechanism that makes sense of metaphorical expressions and could perhaps explain them, one among many other possible stories and mechanisms.

This condition should not discourage us. Studies of the higher human faculties and human social patterns are the hardest of fields in which to plow for knowledge. These disciplines should really be called the hard sciences, for progress here is slow and painstaking, unlike in other disciplines. On the other hand, from these fields you may harvest a lot of satisfaction, insight and other yields, just by plowing.

CPSIA information can be obtained at www.ICGtesting.com
224061LV00001B/14/P